The Christmas Story
as it will be
FOREVER Told

The Christmas Story

as it will be

FOREVER Told

*God's Graphic Image of a Savior
Who Would Die for His People*

**A Personal Advent Devotional
by Stephen S. Ahokas, DVM**

XULON ELITE

Xulon Press Elite
2301 Lucien Way #415
Maitland, FL 32751
407.339.4217
www.xulonpress.com

© 2022 by Stephen S. Ahokas, D.V.M.

All rights reserved solely by the author. The author guarantees all contents are original and do not infringe upon the legal rights of any other person or work. No part of this book may be reproduced in any form without the permission of the author.

Due to the changing nature of the Internet, if there are any web addresses, links, or URLs included in this manuscript, these may have been altered and may no longer be accessible. The views and opinions shared in this book belong solely to the author and do not necessarily reflect those of the publisher. The publisher, therefore, disclaims responsibility for the views or opinions expressed within the work

Unless otherwise indicated, Scripture quotations taken from the New American Standard Bible (NASB). Copyright © 1960, 1962, 1963, 1968, 1971, 1972, 1973, 1975, 1977, 1995 by The Lockman Foundation. Used by permission. All rights reserved.

Paperback ISBN-13: 978-1-66286-621-0
Ebook ISBN-13: 978-1-66286-622-7

Contents

Introduction ix

First Week of Advent: Hope
The Passover: God's object lesson about a savior who would one day
  die for His people. 1

Second Week of Advent: Preparation
What kind of Child. 13

Third Week of Advent: Joy
The circumstances surrounding Christ's birth,
  and a familiar image 23

Fourth Week of Advent: Love
No greater love: a vivid, graphic image of the Lamb
  dying for His people 37

Introduction

Have you ever wondered why there are two Testaments in the Bible? You know, an Old Testament and a New Testament? Do you ever wonder why the Old Testament and the New Testament seem so different from each other—so foreign to each other? They're both in the same Bible, aren't they? There aren't two different messages in the Bible, are there? What is the relationship between them? I spent decades wondering that very question. That is a very broad puzzle, isn't it? I mean, there are sixty-six books and thousands of verses in the Bible.

There is another puzzle that I have contemplated for decades, and this one is a very narrow puzzle. Out of the entire Bible, it consists of only fourteen verses. I am referring to the circumstances surrounding Christ's birth, recorded in Luke 2:6–19. Although these verses describe for us the most momentous, most widely celebrated and meditated-upon event in history, I feel that the full meaning of them is not commonly understood by the masses. I say that because all the devotions, meditations, and attempts to explain the meaning of these verses I have ever read and heard leave me feeling that God is trying to tell me something more. And I say that because when I was young, knowing little about God, Jesus, and the Bible, there was a single verse in that passage that quickened my heart every time I read it. I didn't know why. I just sensed that there was something there.

As I got to know God better, I began to realize it was the Holy Spirit telling me to pay close attention. I didn't know how to pay attention until I began to learn some Bible study techniques. *But one day I stumbled onto something and began to realize that God doesn't write just words. He writes word pictures.* It's not enough to just read the words. I have to look for and identify the picture that God is painting with the words. Eventually, I began to realize that to understand the full meaning of these verses, I have to understand how and what they spoke to the Jewish people (His people) at the time the event took place. And now, by studying the Old Testament account of the Jewish Passover, a book called *Christ in the Passover* by Ceil and Moishe Rosen, the story of Christ's birth and more of the Bible, with help from the Spirit of God (1 Cor. 2:9–10) along the way, I have gained a new understanding of why God orchestrated the circumstances surrounding the birth of His Son the way He did. Along with that, I discovered that the Old Testament and the New Testament really do relate very well to each other. I discovered that the circumstances surrounding the birth of Christ actually paint a picture of a Savior who would one day die for His people! And finally, by examining the circumstances of His birth together with the circumstances of His death, we can all see a vivid picture of our salvation!

Believing now that there is a facet of the story of Christ's birth that has remained virtually untold in all the meditations and devotions that we ever read and hear, I would like to share my own personal advent devotional, in hopes that I might help you, my reader, prepare your heart for the full meaning of the Christmas season. Though I am not as talented with words as many are, I am praying that what I share here will add an extra special blessing to this and all your Christmas seasons to come—and to all your friends', students', and disciples' Christmas seasons to come. I hope and pray that the picture shared here will make it easier for us all to keep the real meaning of the Christmas season in the season.

First Week of Advent

Hope

*The Passover: God's object lesson about a savior
who would one day die for His people*

Hope: it's what gives us reason for living. It seems hard to imagine how hopeless the people of Israel must have felt while they were living a life of slavery to the Egyptians. For one thing, it lasted some four hundred years. It was the only life that many generations of them had ever known. And it was a hard life, without any chance for advancement or reward for themselves. They lived life at the beck and call of their masters—Egypt. All their toil served to advance the nation of Egypt rather than their own nation. I'm sure they didn't even feel like they were a nation.

But after some 400 years, along came Moses with an unimaginable message. Their God had kept His eyes on them the whole time, and He had a dream for them, a dream of freedom to serve God rather than serving Egypt. Their initial response to Moses alludes to how hopeless they really felt. It was as if freedom from Egypt wasn't even a part of their vocabulary. It wasn't even in their thought life.

- *If you are anything like me, you have a dream for your life that seems way too big to be possible. The pathway there doesn't even exist in your mind. But hold on, now. There is a God who wants passionately to be personally involved in your life.*

Nonetheless, God proceeded to outline His plan through Moses. It was a plan that had no chance of working without God's personal involvement in it. The plan was called the Passover, and it was preceded by nine plagues. People often wonder, "Why nine plagues?" Typically, the answer given is that it was to harden Pharaoh's heart. But there are other things that were accomplished by those nine plagues. First, they served as hard evidence to both Egypt and Israel that the God of Israel was personally involved. Second, they all made a distinction between the God of Israel and the gods of Egypt, demonstrating that the God of Israel was the all-powerful one. And thus, they all made a distinction between Israel and Egypt.

- *God has a dream and a purpose for your life. Your pathway to a life of purpose is to find God's dream for your life. Your dream must mesh with God's dream for you. And that means living a life of involvement with God—even the pursuit of God.*

The tenth plague, however, was very, very different. God had made it clear; *not even Israel would be exempt from the tenth plague, except by the substitutionary death of another, the Paschal lamb (referred to from here on as the Passover lamb).* Any family in the land of Egypt, including the Israelite families in the land of Goshen, that was unprepared would have the life of its firstborn male taken by the plague.

Israel's preparation began on the tenth day of the month of Nisan on the Jewish calendar with each Israelite family's selection of their *most precious lamb*. Once the lamb was chosen, the family was commanded to *keep* it until the fourteenth day of the month. Then, at twilight on that fourteenth day of the month (the eve of the Passover, which would begin at midnight), that precious life was to be betrayed, forsaken, and slaughtered, with its blood being collected in a ditch that had been dug in the ground at the threshold of their home's entrance to preclude water from entering the house through the doorway.[1] A rod of hyssop was then dipped in the pool of blood at the base of the door and used to make a distinct pattern of blood around the home's entrance by striking it against the two doorposts and the lintel overhead (Exod. 12:1–12). Not coincidentally, the pattern of blood left at the doorway would have resembled something like that in illustration 1. God had said that the blood was to be a *sign* for them (Exod. 12:13). The lamb was then roasted and eaten, along with strictly *unleavened* bread.

---

[1] Ceil and Moishe Rosen, *Christ in the Passover,* p. 31; Published 1978 Moody Bible Institute.

THE CHRISTMAS STORY AS IT WILL BE FOREVER TOLD

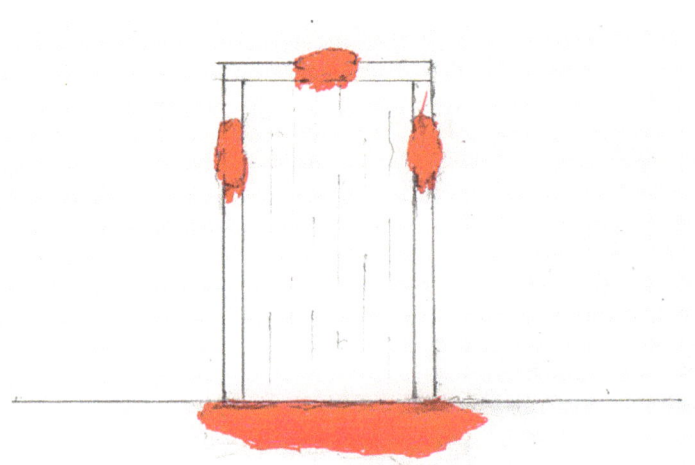

Illustration 1

When the destroyer was dispatched in the middle of the night, God, seeing the sign of the blood of the lamb around the home's entrance, would pass over each home that displayed it, spread His sheltering wings over that home, and prevent the destroyer from entering and executing its purpose in that home (Exod. 12:23). The language in the Hebrew text here is so picturesque that I feel it is worth our while to briefly dwell on it by quoting Ceil and Moishe Rosen in their book, *Christ in the Passover*.

> The verb "pass over" has a deeper meaning here than the idea of stepping or leaping over something to avoid contact. It is not the common Hebrew verb, *a-bhar*, or *ghabhar*, which is frequently used in that sense. The word used here is *pasah*, from which comes the noun *pesah*, which is translated *Passover*. These words have no connection with any other Hebrew word, but they do resemble the Egyptian word *pesh*, which means to "spread wings over" in order to protect.[2]

---

[2] Ceil and Moishe Rosen, *Christ in the Passover*, p. 22

And the Rosen's go on to include Arthur W. Pink's writing in his book, *Gleanings in Exodus,* as he quotes from Urquhart:

> "The word is used . . . in this sense in Isaiah 31:5: 'As birds flying, so will the Lord of Hosts *defend* Jerusalem; defending also He will deliver it; and passing over (pasoach, participle of pasach) He will *preserve* it.' The word has, consequently, the very meaning of the Egyptian word for 'spreading the wings over,' and 'protecting;' and *pesach,* the Lord's Passover, means such sheltering and protection as is found under the outstretched wings of the Almighty. Does this not give a new fullness to those words . . . 'O Jerusalem! Jerusalem!. . . . How often would I have gathered thy children together, as a hen does gather her brood under her wings' (Luke 13:34)? . . . this term *pesach* is applied (1) to the ceremony . . . and (2) to the lamb. . . . **The slain lamb, the sheltering behind its blood and the eating of its flesh, constituted the** *pesach,* **the protection of God's chosen people beneath the sheltering wings of the Almighty**" [emphasis mine]. . . . It was not merely that the Lord passed by the houses of the Israelites, but that He stood on guard, *protecting* each [door displaying the sign of the blood]. [For the Lord will pass through to smite the Egyptians; and when He sees the blood on the lintel and on the two door posts, the Lord will pass over the door and will not allow the destroyer to come in to your houses to smite you (Exodus 12:24).][3]

Thus, each family huddled in such a home was spared. We can say that the *Passover lamb* was effectively, functionally the closest thing

---

[3] Arthur W. Pink, *Gleanings in Exodus,* p. 93; Published by Moody, Publish date not given.

God's people had to a savior who would die for them.[4] Of course, we know from Scripture that, in reality, the Passover lamb fell far short of the Savior they really needed. It could only remind them of their need for a Savior (Heb. 10:1–3).

Knowing that the people would need that reminder, God purposed to establish the Passover sacrifice as a ritual that was to be repeated annually (Exod. 12:14, 25–27). But the Passover wasn't just to be repeated annually. Every year it was to be *observed* (Exod. 12:42). That word *observe* comes from the Hebrew root *shamar,* which means to "watch."[5] By observing or watching it annually, it would serve as that reminder of their need for a true Savior. It would portray a picture of a future Savior who would systematically become etched in the conscience of the people of Israel. It would serve as an *object lesson* about *God's Savior who would one day die for His people.* By *watching it* annually, they would, in a sense, be looking ahead in time and be more likely to recognize the true *Savior* when His time comes. It would remind them that their hope is in the God who would *spread His sheltering wings* over them.

After the last plague hit, Pharaoh literally kicked Israel out of the land of Egypt. Though he later had second thoughts and went out in pursuit, God easily quelled that. And, suddenly, God's people who lived with no concept or hope of freedom from the Egyptians were now free! Suddenly, that group of people whose sole existence was to serve the nation of Egypt was now a nation of people who was free to serve the God who had freed them. (Or so it would seem.)

After they were safely beyond the Red Sea and the Egyptians were no longer in pursuit, God established that annual celebration of the Passover. Yet, it wasn't until after the doubting first generation of Israelites who exited Egypt had passed away and the next generation began to occupy the Promised Land that Israel began faithfully

---

[4] Ceil and Moishe Rosen, *Christ in the Passover,* p. 25, 26

[5] Ceil and Moishe Rosen, *Christ in the Passover,* p. 34

observing the Passover. And observe it they did! By the time of Christ, they had celebrated about 1,200 annual Passovers. Historically, the city of Jerusalem nearly quadrupled in size during each annual Passover week as roughly 2 million people made their annual pilgrimage to Jerusalem for the Passover celebration.[6] Over time and generations, customs and traditions were added to the Passover celebration to embellish it.[7] But its object lesson about a lamb who would die for God's people remained.

By the time of Christ, it was still customary that preparation began on the tenth day of the month of Nisan on the Jewish calendar (the day non-Jewish Christians observe on Palm Sunday), with each family's selection of its most precious lamb. Once the lamb was chosen, the family was commanded to *keep* it in the home and watch it through the fourteenth day of the month. I am convinced that this made the lamb an even more precious life to the family. Ceil and Moishe Rosen in their book, *Christ in the Passover,* insightfully describe it like this.

> The people had to single out from their flocks the handsomest, healthiest looking yearling. An animal of this age, just approaching the prime of its life, was frisky and winsome. Then the family had to watch it carefully for four days before the Passover to make sure it was healthy and perfect in every way. During this period of close observation, they fed and cared for the lamb and grew accustomed to having it around the house. By the end of the fourth day, it must have won the affection of the entire household, especially the children.[8]

---

[6] Ceil and Moishe Rosen, *Christ in the Passover,* p. 42

[7] Ceil and Moishe Rosen, *Christ in the Passover,* p. 40

[8] Ceil and Moishe Rosen, *Christ in the Passover,* p. 25, 26

Again, I am convinced this made the *Passover lamb* an even more *precious* life to the family. Yet, on the fourteenth day of the month (the eve of the Passover), that *dear, precious life* was doomed to be *betrayed, forsaken,* and *sacrificed* the next day. By then the house had been rid of all leaven, and the family had begun eating *strictly unleavened bread.* The significance of the unleavened bread is explained particularly well by Ceil and Moishe Rosen:

> Leaven in the Bible is almost always a symbol of sin. The putting away of all leaven is a picture of the sanctification of the child of God. . . .
>
> In teaching His people this truth, God did not leave them to grapple with abstractions. Leaven was something that every housewife, every cook, used in everyday life. The feel, the smell, the effects of leaven had obvious meaning. The Hebrew word for leaven is *chometz,* meaning "bitter" or "sour." It is the nature of sin to make people bitter or sour. Leaven causes dough to become puffed up so that the end product is more in volume, but not more in weight. The sin of pride causes people to be puffed up, to think of themselves as far more than they really are.
>
> The ancient Hebrews used the sourdough method of leavening their bread. Before the housewife formed the dough into loaves ready for baking, she pulled off a chunk of the raw dough and set it aside in a cool, moist place. When it was time to bake another batch of bread, she brought out the reserved lump of dough. She then mixed the old lump into the fresh batch of flour and water to leaven the next loaves, again setting aside a small lump of the newly mixed dough. Each "new generation" of bread was organically linked by the common

yeast spores to the previous loaves of bread. The human race bears this same kind of link to the sin nature of our first father, Adam.

Often people excuse themselves for bad behavior or wrong attitudes by saying, "I'm only human." But being "only human" is the sin nature within all mankind.[9]

It was customary that every household would bring its Passover lamb to the temple to be sacrificed by the priests on the anniversary of the first Passover. That was the day that began at midnight on the fifteenth day of the month (the anniversary of the day Israel exited Egypt, and the day non-Jewish Christians observe on Good Friday). And at the ninth hour of that day the high priest would climb to the highest pinnacle of the temple and blow the silver trumpet. That trumpet blast would signal the lower priests to begin slaughtering all the Passover lambs. All who were within hearing distance paused what they were doing when they heard it and contemplated the sacrifice that was made.

The people would then take their slaughtered Passover lamb home, roast it, and begin eating their Passover meal (Seder). That meal began the week long feast of unleavened bread. For seven more days after the meal that was eaten at twilight on the eve of the Passover, no leaven was to be eaten.

The death of the Passover lamb on the first Passover gave hope to a people who were told by 400 years of slavery that they had no hope. Now their hope was in an all-powerful God who was personally involved in their life. Every subsequent annual Passover ritual served as a reminder of their hope in that all-powerful God.

So year after year, for about 1,200 years, generation after generation of God's people followed this ritual, *watching the lamb* in celebration of the Passover. And so, the picture that was painted by each

---

[9] Ceil and Moishe Rosen, *Christ in the Passover*, p. 29, 30

Passover celebration became etched in the minds of the nation of Israel. The *Passover lamb* became a familiar figure to all the people. Indeed, it was the *central* figure of the ritual that God had established for His people throughout the Old Testament. Although it fell far short of the Savior they needed, in God's eyes it served well as a vivid picture for His people of the true Savior who would one day come and die for them. The entire Passover sacrifice and the *pseudo savior* or *savior-lamb* who died for them served as God's object lesson to His people about a true Savior who would one day die for them in the future. Literally, that *Passover lamb was effectively the closest thing the people had to a savior who would die for them.*

During the last 400 years of the repetition of this object lesson, there was silence by God, even in the temple. Effectively, Israel was left to her own devices. I find it interesting that the number of years of silence by God was the same as the number of years their ancestors were enslaved in Egypt. Could it be that, in contrast to their 400 years of physical slavery to Egypt, the 400 years of silence was a time when God was teaching an obstinate people something about their slavery to their own sin before He would give them *a heart to know and serve God* (Jer. 24:7)? Could it be that God was still preparing Israel for a life experience that was better than what they had experienced thus far? Could it be that Israel still needed to prepare herself for what God had for them?

- *Jesus said, "**Everyone who commits sin is the slave of sin**" (John 8:34). We should ask ourselves; is there any sin in my life that I need to be freed from? Can I trust God to free me from that sin? He is all of our hope for a life of freedom from sin. In this freedom, we can now serve the God who loves us and wants us to live in intimacy with Him forever.*

Second Week of Advent

Preparation

What kind of Child?

Now we'll begin looking at the circumstances surrounding Christ's birth recorded in Luke 2:6–19. We will spend the next two readings doing so. After 400 years of silence by God, it came as a *momentous event!* To make sure the stage is set, I point out, it occurred at a time when the closest thing the people had to a savior who would die for them was their *Passover lamb*. It came nine months after a young virgin, Mary, and her husband-to-be, Joseph, were both promised by an angel of the Lord that Mary would conceive and bear the Son of God by the Holy Spirit. It came while the two were on a long journey and found themselves in the city of David—Bethlehem.

Luke 2:6–7
While they were there, the days were completed for [Mary] to give birth. And she gave birth to her firstborn son; and she wrapped Him in cloths, and laid Him in a manger, because there was no room for them in the inn.

Much has been made of the humility that Christ displayed by descending from the glories of heaven to become one of us on this planet. This is the side of the story that we always hear and read about during the Christmas season, and it certainly is true and beautiful. *He is Emanuel—God with us!*

- *Yet, if God is to dwell with us, we must prepare ourselves for that. We should ask ourselves some questions.*

- *Can I see Him?*

- *Can I know Him?*

- *What must I do to prepare myself for life in union with my Creator?*

- *He gave us the answer to that last question, saying, "But seek first His kingdom and His righteousness, and all these things will be added to you" (Matt. 6:33).*

- *Again, He said, "Ask, and it will be given to you; seek, and you will find; knock, and it will be opened to you. For everyone who asks receives, and he who seeks finds, and to him who knocks it will be opened" (Matt. 7:7-8).*

Luke 2:8-9
In the same region there were some shepherds staying out in the fields and keeping watch over their flock by night. And an angel of the Lord suddenly stood before them, and the glory of the Lord shone around them; and they were terribly frightened.

These are certainly remarkable and intriguing circumstances that surround the birth of Christ! I dare say no other baby has ever been born in the midst of circumstances like this! A thought-provoking question comes to mind now. Could it be that the circumstances surrounding Christ's descent to earth reveal who He is, what His role is in His Father's kingdom, and what He will do for us? I believe I have found some things, and over the remainder of this and the next reading I will present them to you.

Luke 2:10–12
But the angel said to them, "Do not be afraid; for behold, I bring you good news of great joy which will be for all the people; for today in the city of David there has been born for you a Savior, who is Christ the Lord. This will be a sign for you: you will find a baby wrapped in cloths and lying in a manger."

This passage contains that single verse that I referred to in my introduction when I said it quickened my heart every time I read it. There is an interesting word in that verse that is a big part of what quickened my heart every time I read it. It is the word *sign*. I find that many Christians today don't like that word *sign*, and their natural inclination is to read over it. Perhaps they assume that signs are not commonly understandable. So they think, "Why try to understand?" They tell me they don't like to look for signs. In fact, some tell me there is something wrong with my faith if I look for signs. A thought-provoking observation, though: the sign *was given* to us. The word *sign* is right there in the text. It's not as though we are looking *for* a sign. Rather, we are looking *at* a sign that has already been given to us. To read over a *sign* that God has given to us seems to me to be poor listening. So let's go ahead and consider the *sign* for a while. I promise, it won't be difficult or painful.

To consider the *sign*, we have to go back to the word in the early Greek manuscripts of the New Testament. That word is *sēmeion*. *Vine's Expository Dictionary of Biblical Words* defines it like this: "a sign, mark. .

. ." And it goes on to define it as more than just a mark. Rather, it "is used of that which distinguished a person or thing from others." Similarly, the dictionary in James Strong's Exhaustive Concordance for the New American Standard Bible defines it as a "distinguishing mark." In other words, the message to the shepherds (and us) is that there are some things about that baby that distinguish Him from others. Since it is used in reference to the baby, Jesus Christ, it seems reasonable to conclude that the sign infers some attributes about Him that *distinguish Him from all others*. It is fun and worth our time to consider what some of those inferred attributes about Jesus might be. Let's explore some of them. We can get to know Him better by doing so. We might even begin to see Him for who He really is.

First of all, it is a clear answer to a question that the whole world should be asking, a question asked by the composer of a beautiful Christmas song, *What Child is This?* The lyrics of the song go on to answer that question, at least in part. He was the child who was sleeping on Mary's lap. He was Joseph and Mary's first baby—a baby boy. That is not all. He was given the name Jesus. And, not only that, He was identified by the angel as *Christ, the Lord*. Furthermore, we know from Matthew's Gospel that He is the only child born of a *virgin* woman, distinguishing Him from all other children borne by Mary, the wife of Joseph, or anyone else. So we know that He is the Son of God.

Back in verses 6-7 we read that Mary *gave birth to her firstborn son; and she wrapped Him in cloths, and laid Him in a manger*. In some translations of the Bible, the cloths are referred to as *swaddling cloths* or *bands*.

A talented artist, Jenedy Paige, while doing research in preparation for creating a Nativity scene, discovered some interesting facts about swaddling bands. She once wrote on her former publisher's website:

> *While we often think of "swaddling bands" as scraps of fabric, showing the poverty of Mary and Joseph, they were actually a big part of Israelite culture. When a woman was betrothed, she immediately began embroidering*

swaddling bands which were five to six inch wide strips of linen that would be embroidered with symbols of the ancestry of the bride and groom. Thus, the bands symbolized the coming together of the two families as one. They also symbolized the integrity of the woman, as she strove to make both sides of the embroidery match exactly, symbolizing to her soon to be husband that she was as good on the inside as she was on the outside. These bands were then wrapped around the hands of the couple at the wedding ceremony. So the bands the Savior was swaddled in may have included the lion of Juda and the stem of Jesse."

Jenedy also points out that one of the references she found in her research suggests that the manger was actually a livestock watering trough (as opposed to a feeding trough) that was carved out of limestone. Whether it was a feeding trough or a watering trough, it stands to reason that it would have been located in a place where livestock dwell.

Jenedy now self-publishes, and all of her writings and creations can be accessed through her website.[10]

So now we can see a lot about His genealogy: that it includes Mary and God Himself, and that He is a descendent of Jesse and is the lion of Judah referred to in Scripture. That's entirely exclusive, isn't it? It distinguishes Him from all others. Furthermore, the angel clearly identifies that baby as the *Savior*. More of the genealogy of Jesus Christ can be read in Matthew 1:1-17.

Although we now know *what child* the angel was referring to, my question persists. Is that all there is to it? Is the genealogy and name of the child really all that God intended to reveal to us about that child? Can we really believe that the God who was able and had in His heart to use the prophets to show us attributes of His Son centuries before His birth would be unable or unwilling to use an angel to show us attributes

---

[10] www.jenedypaige.com

of His Son at the time of His birth? Things like His eternal position and the role He plays in His Father's kingdom, and the role He will play in our own lives?

Evan Wickham performs a newer Christmas song, the title of which expresses my deepest and most persistent question beautifully. The name of the song is, *What Kind of Child*. I believe it is just as important for us to ask what kind of child He was as it is to ask *what child* He was. And I believe it was on God's heart to tell us *what kind of child* He was.

My conclusion is that God was not only able and willing to use an angel to show us such attributes of His Son; *He actually did use that angel to infer to us such attributes of His Son.* If I am right, through the words of that angel, *we can begin to see that Savior for who He really is*. If I am wrong, the things that I am seeing are mere coincidences. But, for me, the things that I am seeing are too consequential to be merely coincidental. I don't believe God allows coincidences in His Word. I believe the words of that angel do, in fact, infer some consequential, extraordinary attributes of that child that go much deeper than His genealogy, and *that distinguish Him from all others*. Let's begin examining some of those inferences right now.

Some people interpret the *sign* (distinguishing mark) to be an inference that Jesus was born a King. My first thought was this would distinguish Him from *almost* all people, but not all people. There were other kings in the world (not the least of whom was Herod, who, out of jealousy, sought to kill the child), but not many. But then I began thinking about a small group of people who lived to the east of where Jesus was born. They were the magi. They may very well have been a remnant of the Jews who were exiled to Babylon by King Nebuchadnezzar and never returned to their homeland seventy years later when others did return. A lawyer named Rick Larson has developed a belief that they were a remnant of people from the lineage of the prophet Daniel, often referred to as the *good magi*. They were astronomers or "star gazers."

In the book of Matthew, chapter 2 we read that they saw stars and constellations that indicated to them that a king had been born.[11] But they didn't think He was just any king. They believed He was the *King of the Jews*, saying to Herod, *Where is He who has been born King of the Jews? For we saw His star in the east and have come to worship Him* (Matt. 2:2).

This gets entirely exclusive because, although there were other Jewish kings, Jesus is the only King of the Jews who went on to fulfill the words of the prophet Zechariah, "*Rejoice greatly, O daughter of Zion! Shout in triumph, O daughter of Jerusalem! Behold, your king is coming to you; He is just and* **endowed with salvation, humble, and mounted on a donkey, even on a colt, the foal of a donkey**" (Zech. 9:9; emphasis mine). These words by Zechariah set Him apart as a *humble* King, too. But it doesn't take the reading of these words by Zechariah to recognize Him as a *humble* King. Virtually everyone who recognizes Him as a King recognize Him as a *humble* King by virtue of the fact that He

---

[11] Until recently, all we could do was speculate about what was there for the magi to see. But now, Rick Larson has employed the same kind of computer software that astronomers and NASA employ to forecast for us future astronomical events and navigate their spaceships and satellites through outer space to show us what was there for the magi to see.

In his DVD presentation, *The Star of Bethlehem*, he explains that it's all possible because, as Johannes Kepler showed us, the movements and position of objects in the sky are *precisely predictable*. Thus, by using Kepler's laws of planetary motion, computers can show us what the sky will look like in the future, and what it looked like in the past, from any vantage point on earth or in space. In his presentation, he uses such computer software to show us what was there for the magi to see (stars, constellations, and the star of Bethlehem) from where they were at the time of Christ's birth and during their journey to find the child. He also shows us what the sky looked like during the hours leading up to and through Christ's crucifixion and death, from the vantage point of where it all took place—Jerusalem. And it fully confirms what the scriptural accounts have told us—solar eclipse, blood moon, and all.

If you would like to see what was there for the magi to see, go to www.bethlehemstar.com and order the DVD presentation by Rick Larson called, *The Star of Bethlehem*.

stooped so low as to be found in a manger—a dusty, dirty, smelly place where livestock dwell.

Not only does this distinguish Him *from all other kings,* it distinguishes Him as a *King Who is **above** all others.* For He is the only One Who will fulfill Zechariah's very next words, *I will cut off the chariot from Ephraim and the horse from Jerusalem; and the bow of war will be cut off. And He will speak peace to the nations; and **His dominion will be from sea to sea, and from the River to the ends of the earth*** (Zech. 9:10; emphasis mine).

Finally, we have to conclude that any inference that baby Jesus was born a King would be true, for He said Himself that He was a King while in conversation with Pilate. *"My kingdom is not of this world. . . . as it is, My kingdom is not of this realm." Therefore Pilate said to Him, "So You are a king?" Jesus answered, "You say correctly that I am a king. For this I have been born, and for this I have come into the world"* (John 19:37).

So now we see an inference that the Savior and baby who was found in a manger on the night of His birth is the *humble* King *over all.* This is by far the most commonly recognized and accepted inference. I can't help but notice, though, that, although the Jewish people were looking for a king to be their Savior, their version of a Savior-king was one who would set them free from Roman rule, not someone who would die for them and set them free from their own sin. Furthermore, Jesus said His kingdom was not of this realm. So that prompts me to ask, is there another facet of the *sign* (distinguishing mark) that infers more about Him? I indeed see something and will present it in the next reading.

In the meantime, in keeping with this week's theme of *preparation;* preparing our hearts for the arrival of our Savior should begin with preparing ourselves to submit to His Kingship over us. Preparing ourselves to make Him Lord of our lives. Prayer seems like a good place to start.

- *Prayerfully consider how you might allow God to dwell in you and let Him write His story in your world, in your time, through you.*

- *Prayerfully consider how you might allow God to use you to influence the world in the future. Ponder what kind of legacy you want to leave in the world. Then ponder what kind of legacy you know God wants to leave in the world. Do the two mesh together well? If not, consider how you need to adjust the kind of legacy you want to leave so that it meshes with the legacy that you know God wants to leave in the world through you. Then prayerfully submit yourself to letting Him write His story through you.*

Third Week of Advent

JOY

The circumstances surrounding Christ's birth, and a familiar image

*L*ast time, I proposed that the circumstances of Christ's birth inferred attributes about Him that distinguish Him from all others, revealing who He is, what His role is in His Father's kingdom, and what His role is in our lives. I said after 400 years of silence by God, His birth came as a *momentous event*. And, to make sure the stage was set, I pointed out that it occurred at a time when the closest thing the people had to a Savior who would die for them was their *Passover lamb*. I further said it came nine months after a young virgin, Mary, and her husband-to-be, Joseph, were both promised by an angel of the Lord that Mary would conceive and bear the Son of God by the Holy Spirit. Finally, I said it came while the two were on a long journey and found themselves in the city of David—Bethlehem.

The next inference by the angel's message that I see is a very intriguing one. It is apparent to me by virtue of three aspects of the story. First, it was by the angel's choice of who would receive the message. Second, it was by where the recipients of the message found the child. And third, it was what the recipients of the message saw when they found the child. Let's review once again the circumstances surrounding Christ's birth and the context of the angel's message.

Luke 2:6–9
While they were [in Bethlehem], the days were completed for [Mary] to give birth. And she gave birth to her firstborn son; and she wrapped Him in cloths, and laid Him in a manger, because there was no room for them in the inn. In the same region there were some shepherds staying out in the fields and keeping watch over their flock by night. And an angel of the Lord suddenly stood before them, and the glory of the Lord shone around them; and they were terribly frightened.

Much has been made about the low socioeconomic status of the shepherds and what a privilege it was for them to be addressed and entrusted with a message from an angel of the Lord. This is the side of the story that we so often hear about, and it is so true and beautiful how God reaches out to those of us in the humblest of circumstances. However, there were other people of low socioeconomic status. For example: fishermen. Why were shepherds chosen instead of fishermen or anyone else of low socioeconomic status? Might there be something about shepherds that God could say more through them than He could say through any other?

The reader who is inquisitive and adventurous enough to shift their focus off the socioeconomic status of the shepherds and directly onto their occupation will instantly see something highly significant. Shepherds were the resident professionals of sheep and *lamb* husbandry. They were the ones who were the most *intimately associated* with sheep and *lambs!* Why do I say they were *intimately associated* with sheep and lambs? Because shepherds spent more time with sheep and lambs than anyone else. In fact, it is well understood that there was such a strong bond between the shepherd and his sheep that the sheep *knew* their shepherd's voice.

Could it be that shepherds were chosen because, of all the people on earth, they would be recognized by the people of the land as the ones who were the most intimately associated with sheep and lambs, and because that intimate association they had with sheep and lambs, combined with the verbal message that the angel was about to deliver, would portray a vivid word picture? To begin pursuing that thought, let's review once again the words spoken by the angel.

Luke 2:10-12
But the angel said to them, "Do not be afraid; for behold, I bring you good news of great joy which will be for all the people; for today in the city of David there has been born for you a Savior, who is Christ the Lord. This will be a sign *[distinguishing mark]* **for you: you will find a baby wrapped in cloths and lying in a manger."**

Last time, we made special note that much has been made of the humility that Christ displayed by stooping so low as to be found in a dusty, dirty, smelly place where livestock dwell. Because of that, virtually everyone makes the observation, what an *inappropriate* place for a King to be found! And virtually all of Christendom views Christ as a *humble* Savior because of that. And rightfully so. Scripture is full of passages about His humility, and it exhorts us to live lives of humility in our hearts as well.

But, if we think outside the box, we can see another side of the circumstance of His being found in that place where livestock dwell. Just like there are two different sides of the same coin, there are two different sides of the circumstance of His being found in a place where livestock dwell. And neither side of the story changes the truth about what the other side says about who He is. The side of the story that I refer to here is a side of the story that has been highly elusive to recognition by Bible scholars, Bible students, and Bible readers in general. So what is this other side of the circumstance of His being found in a place where livestock dwell? While virtually everyone makes the observation, what an *inappropriate* place for a *King* to be found, the more intriguing observation to me is, **what an *appropriate* place for a *lamb* to be found!**

Could it be that the words spoken by the angel to the shepherds infer that baby Jesus was born to fill the role of the closest thing the people had to a savior who would die for them up to that point—the Passover lamb? I believe they do, and since arriving at that conclusion, I have learned some interesting facts that corroborate it.

I was intrigued to learn that the circle of territory immediately surrounding the city of Bethlehem, referred to as *Migdal Eder* (AKA, the *Tower of Eder* or *Tower of the Flock*), is referenced twice in the Bible: first in the account of Rachel's death after giving birth to Jacob's youngest son Benjamin (Gen. 35:21); and again as the future birthplace of the Messiah by the prophet Micah (Mic. 5:2). Even more intriguing and not coincidentally, the Jewish Talmudic writings refer to this territory as a consecrated circle a of territory—a territory in which the residing cattle and sheep were consecrated for the sacrificial system. It was in this territory that a special group of shepherds carefully watched over their flocks of sheep. These men were *Levitical shepherds* who served the sacrificial system by identifying at birth, and then raising and grooming unblemished Passover lambs—lambs that would be eligible for sacrifice during an annual Passover celebration in Jerusalem. It would have been to members of this special group of shepherds that the angel appeared and delivered the message about the birth of Jesus.[12]

Donna Snow participated in a tour of the Holy Land hosted by *Artesian Ministries* in 2018, and she commented about her experience in that territory while on that tour. She posted on their website, *That day in Bethlehem profoundly affected my spiritual journey.* She continued by sharing what she learned about the routine those Levitical shepherds followed when they identified at birth an unblemished lamb that would be eligible for sacrifice as a Passover lamb. *As the sacrificial lambs were born, those Levitical shepherds in the Tower of the Flock would*

---

[12] *The Tower of the Flock*, by Dr. Juergen Buehler, November 22, 2012; International Christian Embassy Jerusalem; www.icej.org.

wrap them in [swaddling] cloths to preserve their unblemished state, she writes, alluding to the significance of baby Jesus, all wrapped by His mother in swaddling cloths.[13] In her post she references another article in which the editor of *Faithwire,* Billy Hallowell, cites a video presentation by Rabbi Jason Sobel explaining this.[14] Hallowell provides a link to a Facebook video presentation in his article where interested parties can watch and listen to Sobel's explanation in detail.[15]

John the Baptist offered conclusive insight into the conclusion that Jesus was born to fill the role of the Passover lamb thirty years after His birth when he saw Jesus approaching, directed the attention of the people around him to Jesus, and said, **Behold [Look], the Lamb of God who takes away the sin of the world!** (John 1:29). And he said it with exclamation. The exclamation mark is right there in the text. That tells us he said it with a high level of excitement and emphasis—probably more excitement and emphasis than we would display if we, along with our young children or grandchildren who have never seen a deer, were passing by a field with a herd of deer in it. We would point to the deer in the field and say, *kids, look at the deer!* And why shouldn't John be excited to point out the Lamb of God? Both He and the people around him knew very well the significance of the *Passover lamb* to the people of God. And John knew that **Jesus was *the* Passover *Lamb* who would take away the sin of the world!**

So the inference that those Levitical shepherds (the ones who were the most intimately associated with consecrated sheep and *lambs*) and we are to recognize is that baby found in a place where livestock dwell was more than just a baby. He was more than just *the King over all,* too. He was a *lamb!* But He wasn't just any old lamb. He was the most

---

[13] *The Lamb Wrapped in Swaddling Cloths (Advent Week 2),* by Donna Snow, December 9, 2018; Artesian Ministries; www.artesianministries.org.

[14] *The Incredible Significance of Baby Jesus Being Wrapped in Swaddling Clothes After His Birth,* Billy Hallowell, Editor; December 14, 2017; Faithwire; www.faithwire.com.

[15] https:/www.facebook.com/myfaithvotes/videos/1520113641357563/

astonishing and precious Lamb of all. He was **the** *Lamb*. Don't misunderstand now. This is not to say that Jesus was born some glorified member of the genus *Ovis*. He was born fully God and fully man. What it says is that He was born to fill the role of all the Passover lambs ever slaughtered, past, present, and future. He was God's very own sacrificial Lamb who would one day be offered up, once and for all, **for the salvation of all mankind** ("**ALL the people**," to quote the angel) at the culmination of a Passover celebration that was yet to come. That means even the Gentiles (anyone who is not Jewish) can be grafted into the family of God (Rom. 11:13–24). It's for all who would accept the gift of salvation by placing their faith (ultimate trust) in Christ.

If I were to paraphrase the message that the angel delivered to those *Levitical* shepherds, I would do it in five simple words. If I were to paraphrase the message to all of us by the picture of the angel delivering that message to those *Levitical* shepherds, I would do it in the same five simple words. **THE** *Lamb* **has been born!** We must remember, 1200 annual Passover celebrations by multiple generations of Jews (1200 repetitions of *observing*—**watching**—God's object lesson about salvation through a lamb who would die for them) had virtually insured that everyone knew the significance of the Passover lamb. By the time of Christ, nothing could speak more clearly to a Jewish person about a Savior who would die for them than a vivid picture of a **precious, unblemished** *lamb*. By then it was just a matter of whether or not the people would recognize the Lamb when they saw it.

Might it be that the real reason there was no room in the inn was that God intended those who were intimately associated with sheep and lambs to find His Son in a place where livestock dwell, in the region where Levitical shepherds (those who were intimately associated with Passover lambs) might expect to find a Passover lamb, all wrapped in swaddling cloths the way they routinely wrapped Passover lambs that they were watching over and grooming? Might it be that that is why the angel addressed that special group of shepherds (the ones the people would recognize as the most intimately associated with Passover lambs) when he gave the *sign,* saying, ***I bring you good news of great joy which will be for all the people; for today in the city of David there has been born for you a Savior, who is Christ the Lord. This will be a sign [a distinguishing mark] for you: you will find a baby wrapped in cloths [the way you have been routinely wrapping Passover lambs] and lying in a manger [in a place where livestock dwell, in the region where a Passover lamb would be found***; emphasis mine]? What could bring more **joy** to a Jewish person than that? What could bring more **joy** to *all of us* than the news that we can all have salvation through God's very own sacrificial lamb?

Luke 2:13-14
"And suddenly there appeared with the angel a multitude of the heavenly host praising God and saying, "Glory to God in the highest, and on earth peace among men with whom He is pleased."

We can recall that Scripture describes salvation for mankind as such a joyful event that it is something into which angels long to look. As the apostle Peter wrote, *"And though you have not seen Him, you love Him, and though you do not see Him now, but believe in Him, you greatly rejoice with joy inexpressible and full of glory, obtaining as the outcome of your faith the salvation of your souls . . .* **things into which angels long to look** (1 Pet. 1:8-12; emphasis mine). Apparently, the delivery of the news of salvation for mankind is something that even the angels in heaven consider a joyous event—an event that they can get excited about! As I read these verses, I envision that multitude of the heavenly host not only praising God and saying, *"Glory to God in the highest . . ."* themselves, but calling us to do the same—even leading us in doing the same, the way a church choir or worship team leads us in praise and worship of God.

So, in light of what we've learned here, those who choose not to explore the *sign* that was given to us are missing a whole lot. And those who interpret the *sign* as merely an inference that God put His hand on the child and said, *this is the one!* are missing a lot, as well. In fact, even those who interpret the *sign* as an inference that He is the humble King over all, and nothing more, are missing a whole lot.

If it was an inference at birth that He was God's *Passover lamb,* it was an inference at birth of why He came to earth. It was an inference at birth of what kind of ministry He would have and what the purpose of His ministry would be. It was an inference that He was *destined at birth* to be as enthusiastically accepted by the crowds as He was on lamb-selection day when He rode into Jerusalem on that colt. It was an inference that He was *destined at birth* to be so grievously betrayed and forsaken on that future Passover eve that the people closest to Him would betray and forsake Him, one betraying Him with a kiss, and the others fleeing or denying they even knew Him. It was an inference that He was *destined at birth* to be so grievously betrayed and forsaken by the nation of Israel that during that future Passover celebration the crowd would vehemently cry out, **"Crucify Him!"** It was an inference that He was *destined at birth* to die the kind of death He died. It was an inference at birth of why He would die that kind of death. It was an inference at birth of what day of the year He would die on. It was an inference at birth of what hour of that day He would die. It may have been an inference at birth of what year He would die in![16]

How many other babies are born into this world with the circumstances surrounding their birth saying so much about them?

Luke 2:15–16
When the angels had gone away from them into heaven, [those Levitical] shepherds began saying to one another, "Let us go straight to Bethlehem then, and see this thing that has happened which the Lord has made known to us." So, they came in a hurry and found their way to Mary and Joseph, and the baby as He lay in the manger.

---

[16] For a better understanding of these events and their chronology referred to here, go to Rick Larson's website, www.bethlehemstar.com, click on *The Study* tab, and read all the way through the chronology.

For the reader who comprehends the sign, the imagery of the story is vivid and extended here. And it speaks enormous volumes. It was well known in Jesus's day that a shepherd would leave his entire flock of sheep to go look for one sheep that had become separated from the flock. The reader who recognizes the sign reads here that the shepherds left their flock to go find a single *lamb*. In this case, however, though they may have done so unwittingly, they left their flock not to go look for a lost lamb, but to go look for the most *astonishing and precious Lamb* they could ever find! As the apostle Peter wrote, *"you were not redeemed with perishable things like silver or gold from your futile way of life inherited from your forefathers, but with precious blood, as of a lamb unblemished and spotless, the blood of Christ"* (1 Pet. 1:18–19).

Yes, the imagery of the story speaks enormous volumes indeed! As Donna Snow so aptly wrote in her article:

> *The spiritual significance [of what they saw] would not have been lost on those Levitical shepherds: Jesus' birth pointed to Jesus as the Messiah, the paschal lamb of God who takes away the sin of the world. God did not make the message of redemption complicated or intimidating. He invited everyone to behold the sacrificial miracle of Christmas in the perfect face of His Son, the Lamb of God, wrapped in swaddling cloths.*[17]

We've all heard the saying, *a picture is worth a thousand words*. God shared with us His word picture. Artist Jenedy Paige has shared with the world her personal rendition of what those Levitical shepherds might have seen when they found that most astonishing and precious *Passover Lamb* who was born to give His life that we might dwell with Him under the protection of His sheltering wings forever. To help you better

---

[17] *The Lamb Wrapped in Swaddling Cloths (Advent Week 2),* by Donna Snow, December 9, 2018; Artesian Ministries; www.artesianministries.org.

visualize the picture that God has painted with His words, I would encourage you to visit her website and view her creation, *Little Lamb*.[18]

A sample of it is provided here, with permission.

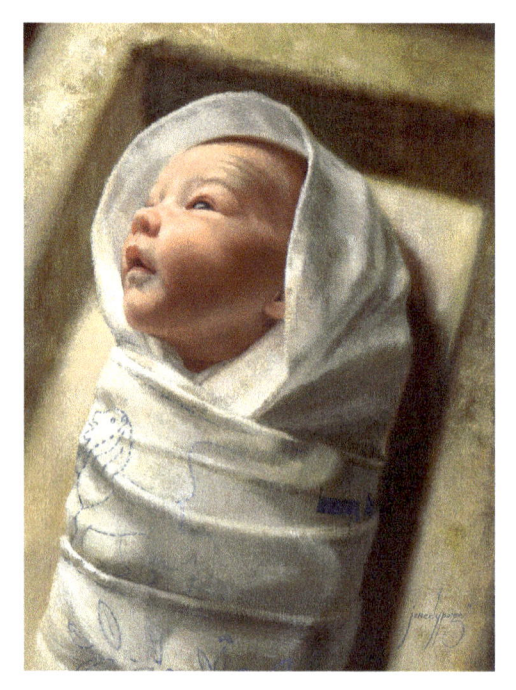

Illustration 2 by Jenedy Paige

Luke 2:17
When [those Levitical] shepherds had seen this, they made known the statement which had been told them about this Child.

For the reader who comprehends the sign, the imagery of the story is vivid and extended still more here. Here we read that the shepherds, the resident professionals of sheep and lamb husbandry, the ones who were the most intimately associated with sheep and *Passover lambs,*

---

[18] *Little Lamb*, by Jenedy Paige, www.jenedypaige.com > Collections > Nativity Collection > Little Lamb

the ones who had the most credentials to speak about Passover lambs, became the first evangelists, telling everyone around them what the angel had told them about this child. Or, rather, to put it in context; began telling the people around them about the most *astonishing and precious Passover Lamb* ever born! Yes, to the reader who comprehends the sign, the vivid imagery in the text indeed speaks *enormous volumes!*

Luke 2:18-19
And all who heard it wondered at the things which were told them by the shepherds. But Mary treasured all these things, pondering them in her heart.

Here, the story suggests that few, if any, of the hearers of it *fully* comprehended the *sign*. But they clearly knew that something extraordinary had just transpired, and that some*one* extraordinary had just been born. And Mary, the mother of the child, in her heart clearly did a lot of earnest pondering about what she had just heard. Yet, if she had *fully* comprehended the *sign,* she likely would not have been quite so distraught at the sight of her son thirty-three years later, all ripped to shreds by a flogging and carrying His own cross through the streets, a cross to which she would soon witness Him being nailed. A cross on which she would witness Him being forsaken, just like all the Passover lambs over the last twelve centuries were forsaken, but in this case, *forsaken even by His own Father in heaven.* A cross on which she would soon witness Him giving up His Spirit.

Jenedy Paige has created another image, this one illustrating the tender relationship between Mary and her newborn baby, Jesus. Once again, to help you better visualize the picture God has painted with His words, I would encourage you to visit her website and view her creation titled, *Delivered.* There you can enjoy Jenedy's touching rendition of that most astonishing and precious of all lambs, all wrapped in embroidered, swaddling cloths, being held by His young mother, perhaps pondering the message that was just delivered to her by the angel through those Levitical shepherds.[19]

A sample of it is provided here, with permission.

Illustration 3, by Jenedy Paige

- *In light of this week's reading, here are some questions you might ask yourself.*

- *Is Christmas a season of joy for you?*

- *What is your **greatest joy** during this and every Christmas season?*

---

[19] *Delivered*, by Jenedy Paige, www.jenedypaige.com > Collections > Nativity Collection > Delivered

JOY

- *Is it that you have another day that you don't have to go in to work?*

- *Is it that you have another holiday to celebrate with others? You know, people greeting each other with smiles and wishing each other, "Happy Holidays?"*

- *Is it snowmen, reindeer, sleigh rides, Santa Claus, and people wearing Santa costumes, winking and saying, "Ho, Ho Ho?"*

- *Is it browsing the stores or internet and contemplating, then purchasing all the shiny trinkets, indulgences, and techno devices that are presented for you to wish for and give to others? New toys to play with? Shiny new luxury vehicles displaying giant, Christmas-colored bows on their roofs, wooing you to splurge? Amazing new electronic devices that will manage your home, finances, car, calendar, and relationships at your verbal or tactile command?*

- *Is it the making, shaping, baking, and sharing of all kinds of decorative, tasty treats with those who are in some way special to you?*

- *Is it decorating the outside of your house with Christmas lights, then driving through the neighborhoods after dark and viewing everyone else's Christmas light displays?*

- *Is it time spent decorating the inside of your home and the Christmas tree together with those you live close to, and then decoratively wrapping all the packages to place underneath the tree?*

- *Is it the thought of receiving all the gifts that you've been dreaming about receiving, and then finally opening them to see which ones have become a reality for you?*

- *Is it time spent reconnecting with ones you want to be close to but live far away from?*

- *Not that there is anything at all wrong with the joys above, but have you come to a point where you can say that your **GREATEST JOY** is that **you now have a Savior** who loves you so much that He was willing to be born to die for you so that you can spiritually connect with Him and dwell with Him in intimate fellowship forever—starting right now, in this life?*

- *You might now be asking, "How can I connect with Him?"*

- *That's what prayer is for. But prayer isn't just speaking words by rote or always asking for things. You can **adore Him** in prayer. You can **confess and repent from sin** in prayer. You can **thank Him** in prayer. And, yes, you can **ask Him** for things in prayer.*

Fourth Week of Advent

Love

---

*No greater love: a vivid, graphic image of the
Lamb dying for His people*

Jesus once said, *Greater love has no one than this, that one lay down his life for his* friends (John 15:13). We've seen some vivid, graphic images of a Savior who would one day die for His people in the circumstances of Jesus's birth. What might we see in the records of the week leading up to His last Passover on earth? To find out, let's follow the Gospel accounts of His experiences during that week and see how they parallel the experiences of all the Passover lambs during the week leading up to Passover. Let's watch it all take place. And, as we do so, let's remember: **His love for us was His whole motivation for being born as one of us and walking through the events of that week.**

Nisan 10, Lamb Selection Day: the day when the most precious, unblemished lambs were chosen to be their family's Passover lamb

It was on the tenth day of the month of Nisan on the Jewish calendar (lamb-selection day, the day non-Jewish Christians observe on Palm Sunday) that Jesus rode into Jerusalem on that colt. And the crowd chose Him loudly, with great enthusiasm. Though they thought they were choosing their king who would free them from Roman rule, they were unwittingly choosing their *Passover Lamb* who would save them from their sin, just like His Father in heaven had chosen Him to be His very own sacrificial Lamb.

> *The disciples went and did just as Jesus had instructed them, and brought the donkey and the colt, and laid their coats on them; and He sat on the coats. Most of the crowd spread their coats in the road, and others were cutting branches from the trees and spreading them in the road. The crowds going ahead of Him, and those who followed, were shouting, "Hosanna to the Son of David; Blessed is He who comes in the name of the Lord; Hosanna in the highest!" When He had entered Jerusalem, all the city was stirred.* (Matt. 21:6–10)

Some of the Pharisees rebuked Jesus and tried to get Him to silence the crowd. He responded with what would seem to be a curious response.

> *Some of the Pharisees in the crowd said to Him, "Teacher, rebuke Your disciples." But Jesus answered, "I tell you, if these become silent, the stones will cry out!"* (Luke 19:39–40)

Such a response isn't so curious after all, in light of the anticipation that all of creation must have been experiencing at that moment. Remember, creation had no culpability in its corruption. That was man's doing. Man's corruption by sin resulted in the corruption of all of creation. Creation's only hope of being set free from corruption was for man to be redeemed. All of creation would have been longing for the moment when it could see Jesus chosen to be the Lamb for the Passover sacrifice. He is the only one who can redeem man.

For the anxious longing of creation waits eagerly for the revealing of the sons of God. For the creation was subjected to futility, not willingly, but because of Him who subjected it, in hope that the creation itself also will be set free from its slavery to corruption into the freedom of the glory of the children of God. For we know that the whole creation groans and suffers the pains of childbirth together until now. (Rom. 8:19–22)

Twilight, Nisan 14, the eve of the Passover: the anniversary of the moment when all the precious Passover lambs were betrayed, forsaken, and slaughtered for the original Passover in the land of Egypt; the moment when betrayal and death was imminent for all the precious Passover lambs ever since that original Passover in Egypt

Just four days after the lambs were chosen, at twilight on the eve of the Passover (the evening that non-Jewish Christians observe on Maundy Thursday), the moment when all the precious Passover lambs over the last 1,200 years were marked for imminent betrayal and death, Jesus, the Lamb of God and His twelve closest disciples ate their Passover Seder in the upper room. It was the meal referred to by non-Jewish Christians as the last supper. As they ate together, Jesus had already been marked for death by one of those twelve, Judas, who had agreed to point Him out to His would-be captors for thirty pieces of silver.

When the hour had come, He reclined at the table, and the apostles with Him. And He said to them, "I have earnestly desired to eat this Passover with you. . . ." And when He had taken some bread and given thanks, He broke it and gave it to them, saying, "This is my body which is given for you; do this in remembrance of Me." And in the same way He took the cup after they had eaten, saying, "This cup which is poured out for you is the new covenant in

> *My blood. But behold, the hand of the one betraying Me is with Mine on the table."* (Luke 22:14–21)

Later that night, while out in the garden of Gethsemane, He was betrayed into the hands of His captors with a kiss by Judas—one of the twelve who were closest to Him.

> *Judas, one of the twelve, came up accompanied by a crowd with swords and clubs, who were from the chief priests and the scribes and the elders. Now he who was betraying Him had given them a signal, saying, "Whomever I kiss, He is the one; seize Him and lead Him away under guard." After coming, Judas immediately went to Him, saying, "Rabbi!" and kissed Him* (Mark 14:43–45). *But Jesus said to him, "Judas, are you betraying the Son of Man with a kiss?"* (Luke 22:48)

Jesus then spoke to His captors, and the remainder of those closest to Him forsook Him, one denying he even knew Him, and the others fleeing the scene.

> *At that time Jesus said to the crowds, "all this has taken place to fulfill the Scriptures of the prophets." Then all the disciples left Him and fled. Those who had seized Jesus led Him away to Caiaphas, the high priest, where the scribes and the elders were gathered together.* (Matt. 26:55–57)

> *But Peter was following Him at a distance as far as the courtyard of the high priest, and entered in, and sat down with the officers to see the outcome. Now Peter was sitting outside in the courtyard, and a servant girl came to him and said, "You too were with Jesus the Galilean." But he denied it before them all, saying, "I do not know*

what you are talking about." When he had gone out to the gateway, another servant-girl saw him and said to those who were there, "This man was with Jesus of Nazareth." And again he denied it with an oath, "I do not know the man." A little later the bystanders came up and said to Peter, "Surely you too are one of them; for even the way you talk gives you away." Then he began to curse and swear, "I do not know the man!" (Matt. 26:58, 69–74).

Nisan 15, Passover day: the day that began at midnight; the anniversary of the day Israel exited Egypt; the day when all the precious Passover lambs were doomed to be slaughtered by the priests.

It was on Passover day (the day that non-Jewish Christians observe on Good Friday) that everyone took their Passover lamb to the temple to be slaughtered. The prophet Isaiah said of Jesus centuries before His arrest and trial, *"Like a **lamb** that is led to slaughter, and like a sheep that is silent before its shearers, so He did not open His mouth"* (Isa. 53:7; emphasis mine).

During the night the religious leaders staged a mockery of a trial.

> *The high priest stood up and said to Him, "Do you not answer? What is it that these men are testifying against You?" But **Jesus kept silent*** (Matt. 26:62–63a; emphasis mine)

> *The high priest stood up and came forward and questioned Jesus, saying, "Do you not answer? What is it that these men are testifying against You?" But **He kept silent and did not answer*** (Mark 14:60–61; emphasis mine)

After declaring Him guilty in their own opinions they brought Him to Pilate.

> *And while He was being accused by the chief priests and elders, **He did not answer**. Then Pilate said to Him, "Do You not hear how many things they testify against You? And **He did not answer him with regard to even a single charge**. . . ."* (Matthew 27:12–14; emphasis mine)

> *Then Pilate questioned Him again, saying, "Do You not answer? See how many charges they bring against You!" **But Jesus made no further answer;**. . . ."* (Mark 15:4–5; emphasis mine)

Being afraid and wanting to release Jesus but not wanting to cause a disturbance himself, Pilate sent Him to Herod for questioning.

> *Now Herod was very glad when he saw Jesus; for he had wanted to see Him for a long time, because he had been hearing about Him and was hoping to see some sign performed by Him. And he questioned Him at some length;* ***but He answered him nothing*** (Luke 23: 8–9; emphasis mine)

Herod, having refused to pronounce judgment on Him, sent Him back to Pilate.

> *The Jews answered [Pilate], "We have a law, and by that law He ought to die because He made Himself out to be the Son of God." Therefore when Pilate heard this statement, he was even more afraid; and he entered into the Praetorium again and said to Jesus, "Where are You from?" But **Jesus gave him no answer*** (John 19:7–9; emphasis mine)

Pilate and Herod both were ready to release Jesus, but now, on the very day when all the precious, forsaken Passover lambs were doomed for slaughter, the crowd—the corporate nation of Israel—forsook Him (that most precious, unblemished Lamb of all) and gave Him up for slaughter. They cried out vehemently for Him to be crucified in the place of Barabbas, an insurrectionist and murderer.

> *Pilate summoned the chief priests and the rulers and the people, and said to them, "You brought this man to me as one who incites the people to rebellion, and behold, having examined Him before you, I have found no guilt in this man regarding the charges which you make against Him. No, nor has Herod, for he sent Him back to us; and behold, nothing deserving death has been done by Him. Therefore I will punish Him and release Him." [Now he was obliged to release to them at the feast one prisoner.]* **But they cried out all together, saying, "Away with this man**, *and release for us Barabbas!"* (He was one who had been thrown into prison for an insurrection made in the city, and for murder). *Pilate, wanting to release Jesus, addressed them again,* **but they kept on calling out, saying, "Crucify, crucify Him!"** *And he said to them the third time, "Why, what evil has this man done? I have found in Him no guilt demanding death; therefore I will punish Him and release Him."* **But they were insistent, with loud voices asking that He be crucified. And their voices began to prevail**. *And Pilate pronounced sentence that their demand be granted. And he released the man they were asking for who had been thrown into prison for insurrection and murder, but he delivered Jesus to their will* (Luke 23:13–25; emphasis mine)

Realizing that the crowd had forsaken Jesus, Pilate had Jesus scourged and handed Him over to his soldiers to take Him away and crucify Him. The soldiers mocked Him and abused Him in various ways, along with twisting together a crown of thorns and putting it on His head. Finally, they led Him away and crucified Him.

> *Then he released Barabbas for them; but after having Jesus scourged, he handed Him over to be crucified. Then the soldiers of the governor took Jesus into the Praetorium and gathered the whole Roman cohort around Him. . . . And after twisting together a crown of thorns, they put it on His head, . . . and led Him away to crucify Him.* (Matt. 27:26–31)

Jesus hung on that cross from the third hour of the day to the ninth hour of the day. With His scalp bleeding after being pierced by a crown of thorns, and His hands and feet bleeding after being pierced all the way through by the nails that held Him to the cross, His figure would have displayed in full view of bystanders a pattern of blood resembling the sign of the blood spoken of in Exodus 12:13, 22 when instructions for the original Passover were given.[20] See illustration 4 and note the similarity to illustration 1 in the first week's reading.

---

[20] Ceil and Moishe Rosen, *Christ in the Passover*, p 31, 32.

Illustration 4

Jesus endured that excruciating six hours of torture with little complaining. Rather than complaining, He prayed to His Father that He would forgive His torturers because they did not know what they were doing.

> *But Jesus was saying, "Father, forgive them; for they do not know what they are doing"* (Luke 23:34).

He spoke to His mother and one of His disciples.

> *But standing by the cross of Jesus were His mother, and His mother's sister, Mary the wife of Clopas, and Mary Magdalene. When Jesus then saw His mother, and the disciple whom He loved standing nearby, He said to His mother, "Woman, behold, your son!" Then He said to the disciple, "Behold, your mother!"* (John 19:25–27).

He even spoke to and forgave one of the criminals that was crucified alongside Him.

And He [Jesus] said to him [the criminal], "Truly I say to you, today you shall be with Me in Paradise" (Luke 23:43).

The ninth hour of Nisan 15: the culmination of every annual Passover celebration on Passover day; the very hour when all the precious, forsaken Passover lambs began dying

At the ninth hour of Nisan 15 (the day non-Jewish Christians observe on Good Friday), the very day and hour when the high priest blew the trumpet, signaling the commencement of the slaughter of all the betrayed and forsaken Passover lambs, the very trumpet blast that prompted all its hearers to pause what they were doing and contemplate the sacrifice that was made, **Jesus entered into the most excruciating experience that He would ever endure.** It was at that moment that His very own Father forsook Him and turned His back on Him. For the first time in eternity He was separated from His Father. Thus, in stark contrast to His gracious plea for forgiveness for His torturers, His gracious forgiveness of a criminal at His side, and His exhortation to His mother and disciple, He cried out with a loud voice, **"My God, My God, why have you forsaken Me?"**

At the ninth hour Jesus cried out with a loud voice, "ELOI, ELOI, LAMA SABACHTHANI?" which is translated, "MY GOD, MY GOD, WHY HAVE YOU FORSAKEN ME?" (Mark 15:34)

About the ninth hour Jesus cried out with a loud voice, saying, "ELI, ELI, LAMA SABACHTHANI?" that is, "MY GOD, MY GOD, WHY HAVE YOU FORSAKEN ME?" (Matt. 27:46)

LOVE

- *Pause now, and contemplate the demeanor of Jesus when He was being nailed to the cross and then during the six hours that He hung on the cross. To us, the pain of crucifixion would be unbearable. In fact, our word excruciating is derived from the word crucifixion. In our minds, crucifixion would seem to be the most excruciating experience Jesus could ever endure. The agitation that He exhibited, the blood that He sweat, and His prayer to His Father that this cup might pass while He was in the Garden of Gethsemane demonstrated that He understood how excruciating the physical pain was going to be. Yet, while it was happening, He prayed to His Father and asked Him to forgive His torturers. He forgave a criminal at His side, and He spoke to and exhorted His mother and one of His disciples who were standing by.*

- *Now, contrast that demeanor with His demeanor at the ninth hour, when all the Passover lambs began dying* **and His Father forsook Him—THE Passover Lamb. He cried out to His Father Who had turned His back on Him! Separation from His Father was even more excruciating than the physical pain He had been enduring up to that point.**

- *What does the contrast in demeanors say about how close Jesus was to His Father during His thirty-three year ministry on earth? Even during what He endured being nailed to and hanging on the cross for six hours?*

- *What might that say about your closeness or lack of closeness to God? Have you reached a point of realization that separation from God is the most excruciating experience you could ever endure? Even more excruciating than physical pain? What do you think makes or would make separation from God so excruciating? What would separation from God be like? Might there be an unexplainable, unrelenting bitterness in the soul? Might there be a conscious awareness of separation from and a deep, deep hunger and thirst for intimacy with the most significant of all others?*

And so that dear, most precious, forsaken Lamb of all gave up His spirit at the very hour when all the people heard the familiar, customary blast of the silver trumpet that signaled the commencement of the sacrifice of the Passover lamb.

> *After this, Jesus, knowing that all things had already been accomplished, to fulfill the scripture, said, " . . . It is finished!" And He bowed His head and gave up His spirit.*
> (John 19:28a, 30)

- *Pause for a few moments, close your eyes, and imagine you are watching a world championship fighting match. Immediately after the match is over, the referee declares one fighter the victor and champion by lifting the victor's wrist high over his head. When the referee lets go of his wrist,* **the victor becomes highly animated and boastful in front of the spectators, celebrating the fact that he is the champion!**

- *Now close your eyes once again and imagine a very different scene—the scene of the brutal spiritual battle at the cross. To the spectators, the one who is supposed to be the victor looks like He is on the verge of defeat in every way. His flesh has been ripped to shreds by a brutal flogging. And for the last six hours, His body has been seen nailed to and hanging from a wooden cross.*

- *Surely the wooden sign bearing the name "King of the Jews" nailed to the vertical post over His head **is an oxymoron**! On the verge of death, He has been heard saying, **"It is finished."** And now He has been seen giving up His spirit. He is dead, and the enemy is the apparent victor. **Nonetheless, with His words, "It is finished," He claimed the victory for Himself. And, yes, He is the victor. He has accomplished what He was born to do—die for His people. And three days later He would be proven the victor by rising from the dead.***

And thus, we have the completed, vivid picture of that Lamb who was born and found in a place where a Passover lamb would be born and found accomplishing what He was born to do—die for His people. If even just one person who was present three years earlier when John the Baptist exclaimed of Jesus, *Behold, the Lamb of God who takes away the sin of the world!,* was present as a bystander, gazing up at Him on that cross, hearing the trumpet blast that signaled the slaughter of the Passover lamb, and witnessing Him giving up His spirit, perhaps they would have recognized the sign of the blood. Perhaps they would have made the connection between that and the trumpet blast. Perhaps they would have contemplated the sacrifice that had just been made. Perhaps they would have finally recognized that the most excruciating experience they could ever know is that of separation from God, both in this life and eternity. Perhaps they would have recognized what the apostle Paul recognized when he wrote to the Corinthians: **"For Christ our Passover . . . has been sacrificed"** (1 Cor. 5:7) and become a new person with a new heart to know God (Jer. 24:7), safely positioned under the sheltering wings of the Almighty for all eternity, beginning not just after death, but right at that moment. If so, they would have positioned themselves in the same place as the families who were positioned under His sheltering wings while huddled in their homes that displayed the sign of the blood of the Passover lamb on their entrances in the wee hours of that first Passover day when the destroyer was carrying out his mission throughout the land of Egypt.

Whether or not there was such a person, I am convinced that Jesus would have considered it all worth it. For that is why He was born in the first place. It was His passion. As He once said in an impassioned statement while overlooking Jerusalem, **"O Jerusalem, Jerusalem, . . . ! How often I wanted to gather your children together, just as a hen gathers her brood under her wings, and you would not have it!"** (Luke 13:34).

- *Jesus once said, "Greater love has no one than this, that one lay down His life for His friends" (John 15:13). Knowing that He fulfilled His purpose for being born by laying down His life for you, how would you respond to Him?*

- *Would you in your spirit turn to Him and say, "Thank you so much! I choose to live with You forever and live the life that You have for me to live, starting now and continuing forever?"*

- *Would you place your ultimate trust in Him to live His life through you and preserve you forever?*

LOVE

- *Look at Illustration 5. As you do so, keep this in mind. It's not so much a matter of choosing whether you want to go to heaven or not. It's a matter of choosing **who** you want to spend eternity with. It's not a place. It's a **Person**.*

Illustration 5

- *Jesus once said, "**These things I have spoken to you, so that in Me you may have peace. In the world you have tribulation, but take courage; I have overcome the world**" (John 16:33). Knowing that we can all expect difficult trials and tribulation in this life, some of them potentially life or death situations, is there any more secure place you could be in this world than under the **outstretched, sheltering wings of Almighty God**?*

- *Is there any more secure place you could be throughout eternity than under the **outstretched, sheltering wings of Almighty God**?*

- *Think of the study of the word Passover that we looked at in the first week's reading. At the same time, think of the prophet Isaiah's expression in Isaiah 31:5, **"Like flying birds so the LORD of hosts will protect [you]. He will protect and deliver [you]; He will pass over and rescue [you]."** If you are positioned under the sheltering wings of almighty God through the death of that most precious of all Passover Lambs, when your temporal life comes to an end, whether in a timely fashion or an untimely fashion, you will be **preserved**! Is there any position you would rather be in, both in this life and eternity?*

We've been looking at and discerning some vivid word pictures throughout this devotional, and we've come to the point where we see not just the picture of our salvation, but the picture illustrating God's intended *result* of our salvation. Although all the work that was needed to accomplish our salvation was accomplished by Christ's death on the cross, the picture of our salvation isn't done there. Our salvation isn't a snapshot or still picture. It is better described as a motion picture. Let's remember, although the ninth hour of Passover Day and the sacrifice of the Passover lamb were the culmination of the Passover celebration, they were only the beginning of the week-long Feast of Unleavened Bread.

In the first week's reading of this devotional we read at the bottom of page 6 and the top of page 7 of their book, *Christ in the Passover*, Ceil and Moishe Rosen's very vivid explanation of leaven's representation of sin. The *week-long* feast of *unleavened* bread that began at the culmination of the Passover serves as a vivid, pictorial representation of the intended, sweet, sinless life that begins with repentance at the foot of the cross and persists as the *life-long* living out of our salvation. As the Rosen's continued in their book:

> The apostle Paul, in 1 Corinthians 5:6–8, spoke of leaven as pride, malice and wickedness. He said, "Purge out therefore the old leaven, that you may be a new lump [a new person] as ye are unleavened [cleansed]. For even Christ our Passover is sacrificed for us."
>
> On the other hand, Paul described the *un*leavened bread as sincerity and truth. The Hebrew word *matzo* (unleavened) means "sweet, without sourness." The unleavened bread typified the sweetness and wholesomeness of life without sin. It foreshadowed the sinless, perfect life of the Messiah, who would come to fulfill all righteousness and to lay down His life as God's ultimate Passover Lamb.
>
> Thus, for the Hebrews, the putting away of all leaven symbolized breaking the old cycle of sin and starting out afresh from Egypt to walk as a new nation before the Lord. They did not put away leaven *in order* to be redeemed; rather, they put away leaven **because** they were redeemed. This same principle applies to the redeemed of the Lord of all the ages. Salvation is of grace, "not of works, lest any man should boast" (see Eph. 2:8–9).[21]

---

[21] Ceil and Moishe Rosen, *Christ in the Passover*, p 30.

- *Does the life-long living out of a sweet, sinless life seem like an impossibility to you? Well, if we are honest, it is impossible, in a natural sense. We are all only human, and all humans inherited a fallen nature. But don't let that discourage you. God understands that, and that is why He sent His Son, Jesus, to earth to die for us.*

- *It was out of perfect love for us that Jesus accepted the assignment of being **born into this world to die for us**. When we choose to live with Him forever, tell Him that we want to do so, and then place our ultimate trust in Him to make it happen, we are adopted into the family of God. We become a child of God.*

- *Just like our own children have to learn incrementally how to walk, we, as children of God, have to learn incrementally how to walk in God's ways.*

- *I once heard an insightful definition of walking. It is the act of continually falling and catching oneself. When God shows us our sin, we agree with Him that it is wrong. We catch ourselves and change course.*

- *Bill Bright, the founder of "Campus Crusade for Christ," called it spiritual breathing. We exhale the bad (confess – agree with God that it is wrong), and inhale the good (agree with God that His ways are good and walk in them).*

- *To put it another way, it's not as though we never fall into sin. But we don't practice sin to become good at it, either. When we fall into sin, we get up again. The **discernment** and **power** to do so comes only through **faith in Him**. Thus, **through faith in Him, we can begin living a supernatural life.***

Here is my prayer for us all during this and every Christmas season: Lord, May we make You our **greatest Joy** throughout this and every Christmas season. May we be like the *"myriads of myriads, and thousands of thousands [of angels], saying with a loud voice, 'Worthy is the LAMB that was [born and then] slain to receive power and riches and wisdom and might and honor and glory and blessing'"* (Rev. 5:11b-12). And may we be one of *"every created thing which is in heaven and on the earth and under the earth and on the sea, and all things in them, . . . saying, 'To Him who sits on the throne, and to the LAMB, be blessing and honor and glory and dominion forever and ever'"* (Rev. 5:13).

Merry Christmas!